SHERWOOD FOREST

FUTUREPOEM BOOKS

NEW YORK CITY

2011

SHERWOOD FOREST

CAMILLE ROY

FIRST EDITION | FIRST PRINTING

This edition first published in paperback by Futurepoem books
P.O. Box 7687 JAF Station, NY, NY 10116
www.futurepoem.com

Executive Editor: Dan Machlin
Editors/Production: Chris Martin, Jennifer Tamayo
Guest Editors: Eileen Myles, Bob Perelman, Kim Rosenfield

Cover design: Mickel Design (www.mickeldesign.com)
Typesetting: HR Hegnauer (www.hrhegnauer.com)
Typefaces: Custom Font by Mickel Design (Spine & Back Cover); Sabon (Text)

Printed in the United States of America on acid-free paper

State of the Arts

NYSCA

This project is supported in part by a grant from the New York State Council on the Arts, a state agency, as well as by individual donors and subscribers. Futurepoem books is the publishing program of Futurepoem, Inc., a New York State-based 501(c)3 non-profit organization dedicated to creating a greater public awareness and appreciation of innovative literature.

Distributed to the trade by Small Press Distribution, Berkeley, California
Toll-free number (U.S. only): 800.869.7553
Bay Area/International: 510.524.1668
orders@spdbooks.org
www.spdbooks.org

Any book is the product of a context but this one seems particularly so. This is a San Francisco text. The Bay Area writing scene has been a rich source of friendships and intellectual life. So many people here have nourished and guided my writing. I am grateful for their influence, their work, and for our collective enterprise. I would like to especially thank Robert Glück for making me a better writer, and for all the dimensions of our long association.

This book is dedicated to the memory of three friends who were supportive of the work in progress: kari edwards, Steve Gleason, and Scott Maynard.

My Play 3

Ideology 5

Cinderfella 7

Boxy 9

Bleeding the Lizard 10

Snow Instruction 11

Marching Band 13

The Tower Hotel 14

Sacrifice It 16

Diary of 3 words

April 14 (Tuesday): Trash 17

April 28 (Monday): Beauty 18

May 3 (Sunday): White 20

Red Hood 22

Dorothy, Near the End 24

Crime Story 28

Arabian Stud 34

Lucy in the Sky 36

La Fica È Sacra 43

History of the Slut in My Relationship 46

Wanting to Register in the Road & the Characteristics of the Real 48

Embarrassed Tract 50

Keeping a Chewy Grippe 51

The Royan Hotel 53

Golden Syrup 55

Cold Virgins (a Sad Song) 57

Lucky Fortune Is Good 59

Film Loop 61

Princess & Salt (a Ballad) 63

Properties of Criminal Girls in the String Universe 65

Today 67

Torture in Dapple 68

Sing Song 69

Artifact 71

Parade 73

Revolt is its bread, its exclusive respiration, its soil.
From this evolves its sinews, its glinting explorational fiber.
This being the mode of its disruptive English,
its anti-memorials, its slow motion lightning . . .

—Will Alexander,
"Singing in Magnetic Hoofbeat"

I'm bound for Black Mountain, me and my razor and my gun.
Gonna cut him if he stands still and shoot him if he runs.

—J.C. Johnson,
"Black Mountain"

SHERWOOD FOREST

MY PLAY

You are dead, imagine it.
So I should speak as one possessed,
grim & miraculous. Your word startles
the process: killer.

. . . The unborn occupy the dead, like some relationships.
Still, the appalling, almost feverish discomfort we cause each other—
this is our science story, which I place
in the safe deposit box of your butch heart.

Our audience arrives as voyeurs with a wish, a natural desire
to be transformed into masochists. Not because they want to be
overwhelmed by suffering; quite the contrary. They seek an actual
possibility, not an actualized one.
Yet they suffer from the fact that the body is effeminate (that the asshole
is speaking).
This isn't shit, it's poetry.
Shit enters into it only as an image.

. . . My rather elastic neck droops, hips flatten, skeleton begins its grin.

But it has a bad smell, this play: the aroma of *nothing happening.*
Then I become aware of the theatrical quality of sex shows, porn, politics.
"The show" is everywhere. Theater is a quality
not a place.

. . . I want to write Eileen but I'm feeling guilty, I'm too high.

I fold my muscles into wads and sleep soundlessly.
I can't remember my dreams, they crumble, a soft cake.
A picnic with Carla. She brings rosemary bread and surprising pistachios.
She reads to me about utopias.
So touched and happy I float right up into the sky.

IDEOLOGY

Every virtue has its contemptible literature.
—Céline

1989. I was looking for an instruction. I walked with silent multitudes towards the sobering event, where I found Amy at the podium, grasping every straw and shaking her hairy head in terror.

Like pillows in chaos

Amy's clever speech inserted itself into the fields of young cervix. As each point arrived, tiny holes among us bridged the gap between *futile* and *fertility*.

Humbly, I placed my feet a few inches further apart. Although I'm shallow I couldn't swallow. Yet, at the proper point, as marked by the separated passages of text, I did go inside. The herd was waiting for me there—big girls lathered in their flesh, crushed with insider love. They married me with their lips. I named myself Amy, then made my own series of stirring announcements.

Walking. Walking out. Walking in. The Amy crowd just stood around, waiting for me. But I was waiting too, which is why I couldn't arrive. I was looking for something pointy, yet blank, that wore a pout the way I wore the names of my friends. I needed to get into the interior, so I could look for this thing: call it cervix. It seemed I waited forever. Finally, I was told it had popped and disappeared, a sort of dispirited ghost.

That's when you rolled up, Dick. What a welcome distraction in our dusty rest stop, with ironic scenery, a Plymouth in our Valiant field. But you were so terribly sleepy. In fact, you were dead! Yours was a belief system that attached sweetness to events.

(Which should have meant something to me. Punched, somehow.) We gathered in the cloakroom, laying you in the center, in piles like rope. It turned out there were many ways to take off the outer coverings, and the kneecaps followed. O Dick, everything liquefied after the first dark and sparkling moments.

Now I want to make a poem of it, this time with caricature. Dick, you be the big jaw, and I'll be minnows, pushed out between your ivory teeth, while Amy holds us in her thick romantic fur.

Then, getting off, daddy-o, finally getting off. Your spreading butt —why so huge and cracked? It must be the beyond, where you are. (Where I wanted to go.) Infested abstract landscapes have *Dick* written all over them.

Pure dream of momentum, soaring from the hard kick towards the value of an image, as panorama foams while I'm asleep.

Dick, wake up please. I'm really ready for you to wake up.

CINDERFELLA

We know the story:
Cinderfella locked in a tower with her terrific long hair.
Somebody climbed it (a hag, the hair).
Brought her chips & dip daily, until
one day
got mad &
chopped it.
I mean the
post-menopausal hag
cut off her mane.
Now she's Girl Dude.
Check the roll to his tiny hips.

Did you know Cinderfella swallowed her pagan prince
before she ran off into the wilderness?
His gentle melancholy became her.
His moustache also
sprouting to the Left & Right
copious, earthward, in delicate curls,
as Cinderfella sprinted through the forest,
hooves of a sex kitten crushing herbs,
bearing a gelatinous halo—
Hir transparent dime;
call it gender, or crown.

When Cinderfella became a boy
her tongue leapt from his heart,

the red flag of the new kingdom.
We enter its dark tunnel every day.
We have to, to get to work,
stopping for soldiers & checkpoints
as we stumble over those
voyeurs called words.

Outside, upstairs in the air
Cinderfella swoops, a dove
with antlers,
okay? I mean,
it's beautiful at night,
when the demon holds the sacred bone
and all bodies fall into the fella,
whose chest is broken open &
sucking us in.

BOXY

The genetics counselor said these children are often smart
but she had never heard of one who was *exceptionally* smart.
It was Valentine's Day.
A spiteful little egg burned as it drifted down:
the last one. Unborn.

My friends are shitty, barely there, cool breaths.

My role as host is to change
expressions slowly.
I suggest frameworks
for industry, masquerading as desire.
I know I'm wrong. Wrong is that burn
in my crotch
where delicious wish stirs the red broth:
dimpled white lines head straight for Canada.
The world needs me!

Simone Weil: *Work is like a death. We have to pass through death.*
    We have to be killed . . .
(My toes represent the chewy agreement of my flesh.)

Because I can't see everything, I can only see a few things,
his radiance is nothing more than a remark
heading into the present.
There's a smelly young person in that boxy closet.
I have a concealed weapon
it's my personality
. . . an Irish thug.

BLEEDING THE LIZARD

Chewing the mouth of saying nothing,
in the *way* of that,
I can't attach my feeling to its circumstances.

I show Bob the new poem (the one with lovers X & Y) and he frets.
He wants them to be located, in relation, with real names—their floating
quality is unnerving, or perhaps just not 'sufficiently articulated.' But
you can blot sore areas with swampy love. I believe that.
Then why do I write stories like eroded holes?
Peek through
       see the world . . .
A representational hole: sad gutter in the throat.
My nightmare grazes the stems of idealization
so if I don't move, I might remember sexual bliss.
(How she made me sit still,
which got me so hot I could hardly stand it—felt *ravaged by love*.)
Closing off the small love with no echo,
I scrape my cunt until I come. Yellow flowers more brilliant than lemons.
Banks of fragrance.
Then it's you again, you *mouse*.
No greater misery than meeting your match!

SNOW INSTRUCTION

At dawn their blue and black stripes slid out of the village
in extreme blur: training.
One by one. eyes shut, dropping down the chute,
according to these instructions:
—// Keep each grain in sight until it melts in the pump.
—// Standby while hearts stamp or clamp snow.
—// Make steam out of exhausted breath.

. . . I felt threads because the girls were snow. After all!
From every nest, in the surreal cloud of our girl-home
each hug of speed made nausea pee pee.
O yearning in wads
we slid down ramparts.
       the melancholy bullet girls who twinned my face.
Our collapsed but sweet
  Sweet—//
       melancholy bullets
Soaring—
Blue waves—
  glimmering ice webs   *thousands*
Gulfs   edged with cracked powder.

 (A black body glove
       rubbered at the tips)

Mine *equaled* fat and oily. Her racer blubber—
tastiness so pure & juiced up!
Shambles, tearing
downhill.
She made it to a village—// snow
collapsed there.
I held her dripping mittens.
Breath from her belly steamed the room.
What's the difference, I asked, between what you do, and what we all
    do, secretly, together—she winced & said—
"A girl is a small idol nested in the body. Gnarled & coiling her teeth—"

MARCHING BAND

I got off before girls started getting
their sex change operations.
I didn't stop to look. I got off
with my organs intact. I got off a lot.

I got offered a sex change operation.
and I got one or two, then I gave up
everything but breathing.
I tried the lacy pants, but they itched.

What is a girl, anyway?

THE TOWER HOTEL

Two girls in a bed with fog lather.
Lonnie hauls them from one piss-in-the-sink to another
dodging beards etched in crypto-celtic patterns,
the duds of the syndicate.
The boy is an abandoned paint factory.
Lonnie says they'll leave the city because the girls were threatened.
I know what he means:
Love is a mask applied over discontinuity of moments spent with
    the same person.
Yet if running away is your state of mind
. . . doesn't everything appear to flow away, to a discontinuous mind?

Or edges have a way of making each lose her head . . .
and the girls are just using him for his grasp.
I know Beanpole never says a word. She's mute.
The other one is called Little. They're so cold
in the hallway. Lonnie screams from his mattress
not at them—at us, at everyone.

Fog so heavy the cars in the street
appear to be moving through snow.
Winking pad surfaces
through a raised fabric of blue lights.
The moon geologist spent so much money on us—
how could it have been a false indicator?
My beloved says it all should have been obvious.
She's running away with the truth!

I put my finger on her clit, while she's watching the game.
"May I have your attention, Miss?"
I'm tiresome and not funny, she says.

White throats sweetly jagged from a ragged butch knife dull.
I shall be butching thee from nape to rump.

A scribe of "sensual collisions that express the authority of terms"
—money, butch, whore—
while pulling at a long nipple. Tattoo Blue
digs her fingers into the dancer's fleshy waist—wide red kiss
as patches of green
drift from wallets.
I prefer a part that spits & rolls:
sweet Ramona, as she pumps and sugars the mouth of the logger dyke.
. . . but if you play softball on a Rec League team
everything else is just a dream.

SACRIFICE IT

Sacrifice it, the impulse to sun
then give us our daily

(oh boy)

Scott whispered
he'd copped a script: Vicodin. I nodded, breathless,
& glided on towards my private island, oars in water,
through Japanese animated cloudscape.

The less my writing *weighs* . . .
I can't connect the beginning,
my sensational law.

To do list: fret, hit banks, rob my skin.

DIARY OF 3 WORDS

APRIL 14 (TUESDAY): TRASH

Well, that's weird: TeaJay just got married. To a carpenter with a mullet and he's turned her to Jesus, so I heard. This gives me pangs of regret. It's the death of an interesting body.

When I think of the body as parts—as muscles and skeleton and organs and skin in a swarm—I think of TeaJay. When I knew her, she was a big sullen girl. At the level of the body she seethed and at all other levels she was pretty dumb. Her shoulders were broad and her tits had that creamy excess. They made her top-heavy. She could spin with force. She wasn't fat at all, that's not what I mean. You felt she could tackle you just by falling. TeaJay was a runaway when she showed up at the parlor, I hope she was at least 18. Maybe not, though. I thought she was hot but Scout found that sentiment annoying—she had to work with her, and TeaJay could be a pain in the ass.

TeaJay had a weird relation to language: words entered her and didn't come out. When you said something to her, her face closed and she stared at you with a resentment so deep it was erotic. Once in a while a word made it back out, but it would be irradiated. Like with the jackets. One night TeaJay and Lucy and Scout showed up in athletic jackets which had been custom-made in satin: one peacock blue, one blazing orange, one a lustrous emerald. They glowed in the smoky club. On the backs in big white letters was the word TRASH.

The effect was shocking and beautiful. For years I fantasized that I'd missed out by mistake, that my jacket would appear . . .

There was this skinny guy who used to drop by the parlor and just hang out. He was polite but a little smarmy, bending at the waist, his arm extending out like a claw, holding boxes of chocolates. Suddenly we knew why he was hanging around, a collective moment of insight: pimp fantasies. He was having them. It was TeaJay who set him straight. She told him he had to leave. His face crumpled. He asked why. In that suffocated little girl voice of hers, she half sang, "Why? Because we hate you!"

What can I say? What's the point of this melancholy brain fart. Maybe I should write a poem about it.

APRIL 28 (MONDAY): BEAUTY

Feeling focused, yet too startled to masturbate. I'll masturbate later. Much thought tonight.

After sort of a druggy weekend, we went out to Land's End at sunset. We found a spot where there was a view through the cypresses across the Golden Gate to the Headlands. There we watched the ocean sparkle like the night sky, except it was silvery gray and bosomy and all wrinkled up, like an elderly Mae West.

After the ocean went black we went home and watched *Twin Peaks*. It was an episode in which one of the female characters is tortured and murdered, in long slow takes, with a sound track of muffled thuds. The victim's lips were amazing. So dark & red they looked like pain. Voluptuous hatred seemed to dangle like a intricate Christmas tree snow flake. Its slow twirl *equaled* suspense . . .

> *Thud and Beauty on a date: Oh no! What is the matter with Thud? Why can't he appreciate what he's got? Even the breeze is smug, wafting overhead with a voyeuristic satisfaction as Beauty gets what's coming: Thud's envious hammer.*

The scene ends with sudden dark swamping the camera. It seems daring but really it's looking away at just the moment that blood splashes up and makes such a fucking mess. Men are never bumped off with such relish. After the video was finally over, my beloved snarked that she wanted her own tv show, which she would call *Rebuttal*.

This suffocating cloud. What started it? What is it? Who is to blame? Who is my enemy? I'm pierced by doubt. A line came at me and I wrote it down on my palm: "Envy is the term around which desire pivots."

Envy. Is the term. Around which desire. Pivots.

Beauty: I want her body, too. I want to be inside it. But I don't know how, which makes me feel like a dumb bunny tumbling through the world. I went to the sex toy drawer and got all the handcuffs and laid them out on the bed. Metal handcuffs annoy me. But the furry pair . . . they're so soft . . . I'll sleep in them tonight.

Restraints seem to promise that someday the body will arrive, which means I'm waiting for something real: orgasm confirmation: of belief. I'm still waiting! waiting . . .

MAY 3 (SUNDAY): WHITE

I'm doing things wrong. I missed the phone bill. I had to go down to the office to keep them from turning it off. People think I'm strange. (I think.) What is true? Paranoia has a way of poking out. I took the drugs from Lucy last night and my legs melted. The last time I bought some from her it looked like brown sugar. Something! Raw as brownie mix! Later I took a taxi to go meet Bruce with my thoughts scaling cliffs and so on. I have thoughts on Venus, thoughts in the great rift valley of Mars. The poor fucked up etceteras also bother me, I think they're in my body whenever I do these drugs. My system veers between adrenalin and these most unfortunate thoughts. I couldn't think about meeting Bruce at all, which I should have, in order to be prepared.

All Bruce could talk about was the trouble he'd be in if Leah saw him at the club with me. He said I offended her at the party because I was not attentive enough to her opera descriptions. He delivered this news with relish and then bashfully dropped his lashes. I swung from rage to tears. Now I have enemies in a stream & no one knows this but me. Turned out Leah never showed up at the club but it didn't matter, I'd started crying into my fists, trying to keep the tears out of my mascara.

We sat next to this punk motorcycle chick. The club is so small I was practically in her lap. She kept smiling at me, her enormous eyes spooked me a little. She said she liked my mascara. I said it made the world look like the inside of a snow globe—sparkly plastic snow, because it's *white*. She nodded like she completely understood. Then she got up and went to the mike. She was on the bill! Her name's Kathy Acker. She read poetry, weird but great. That night I had a dream that she bonded with me as another chick, which felt odd because in my dream I was having a fag day, I felt like a big exploding fag, but Kathy Acker came up to me and looked at me (enormous eyes) and said,

In my heart (the location of my most true feeling) I'm a fag too but I'm crawling out of this cunt. Where did I get this cunt?

RED HOOD

Little Red skips through the outback
trailing a red balloon:
I-trial, her floating word.
When she crosses the stream
she falls in.
Tumult under the bridge.

Worlds withdraw from the rushing water.
Names & letters: goners—
with Little Red tumbling after,
to the beat of her grass heart
as all roads disappear
& ruin geometry.
Alone, without politics,
she's swept from mother to night.

My body is every body, she cries,
startling a wolf.
"Your proper being is potential,"
he corrects, taking up a trot
along the shore. Other words
of his bad conscience:
"Poor little chick!
Hiding behind spicy red lips."
(Flapping apart
neither will be saved).

Your house of skin is all wind,
        sings the wolf, as he swims.
My body is every body,
        she cries, again & again.

O tender bite—!
His one accurate art performs
like a tongue, splitting right from left
in flat out songs.
Finally snacking on the grass heart
(even as she still squeals)
he is no longer embarrassed.
Distrust, disconnection, dishonesty—
he licks the dishes. Takes a nap.

Little Red regrets how she did love it
or not exactly.
As reddish puckers, the ballerinas,
melted into her skin, our red
mistress tasted throat burger.
Wolf story gleamed under her cloak.
It was so beautiful, that minute.

DOROTHY, NEAR THE END

Rib cage becoming rib wheat. Liver clover appearing in crumbled dirt. All that sprouting amidst stillness: she recognizes this pattern. What flows from her nostrils fills the silky air. Even so, Dorothy feels the discipline *breath* rumbling through her pasture.

Someone flips the hips on her grammatical mat. Gratefully sinking deeper into its crust, still among soldiers, marching forth and back until all fall down, yawning. Knobs of the interior expose their rotten teeth.

Dorothy rowing gently
down the stream of rosy medals.
Military medals—measuring the distance.

When she finally opens her eyes, children rush out and go from door to door, spreading the news: Dorothy's home.

Auntie, Dorothy says, what am I, these Senses in fur?
And my companions also *lush virgins* just as every stream
rolls downhill?

Dorothy's Did's and Don'ts.

. . . Flow into the street of strange events.

. . . Clamor for their thrill.

. . . Walk and talk with the illness.

Dorothy Tells A Story

—*Have* you heard the story of the old man and the horse?—It goes like this—An old man decided to teach his horse not to eat—Every morning he fed his horse half of what he'd fed him the day before— He finally succeeded in feeding him nothing—A day later he found his horse in his stall, dead—So the old man goes to the rabbi—*Why* did my horse keel over, after I'd just gotten him trained?

—D'ya remember the inside
—Amputated, so we did the next best thing?
—Getting "streetwise," ha ha

—Meant choosing a different hotel.
—One with no doors. Just slabs of wood
—leaned against the openings.

—Dorothy you were so fucking sociable.
—Slap that padlock.
—You told me, One Eye

—to be concerned about. "Cause
—the eye leaks, where the ball is missing."
—So I inspected it. And there you were.

—Sitting on my bed.
—Padlock as large as any knee.
—I didn't think you'd wake up.

—But I was populated, like Poetry
—is populated. Right, Dorothy?

Oh bother. Tinkle thru another episode. It's so period without an
    object. So washed
period. We're inside that little dot, and shrinking. *No place like the
    home place.*

Don't go out there, Dorothy. Get in bed with the phone and breathe
    into the headset.
In that hissing stream, find the funny part.
When I'm yelling it lathers you, upside your head. Don't tell me to
    be quiet.
    Narratives point at moments of violent compression.
    That's what they live for: arriving in a stew of breath.
I'm chicken bones, left in the bottom of the soup pot. So well-cooked
I'm gone. I like to sob for the lost animals in my chest.
You know what they say, Dorothy—"The self is made only of non-
    self elements."
Or else they say, "Speak only for yourself. It's more hygienic."
    Gracious. You're stirring again?
        Tart & cold—a dip stick in lemonade!
        . . . There you go. Up and about.

    I like to lay here, waiting

in this drawer, until you open it. Then suck cool air into the nerves
exposed like knives and forks. *It's all about me.* And you—going
    out again,
so soon? Big head seeming bigger & your soft cloak of dorothy skin.
Two smooth, diligent eyebrows spear my rooms.

CRIME STORY

Ludmilla was 39, at the cusp of the never-married, and her brown hair sprung back from her head in thick vigorous waves. She was wiry and lithe, with a knobby and somewhat oversize nose. As she was showing me around the apartment, she thrust her disconcerting throb of a face close to mine and said with emphasis, "I'm Republican but liberal on homos and abortion."

I don't remember how she knew I was queer, or how I knew she had a room for rent.

She added in a confidential tone, "I'm hoping to get rich through marriage." I nodded as I looked around. I needed a stopover one night a week. It had been Lucy's idea, that we should avoid the motels.

As I stood, listening to Ludmilla, at the door to the bedroom which was for rent, I felt my taste morph into a kind of studious surrealism. First it emptied out in one gush of breath, then everything creamed together: the room, in harvest gold drapes and avocado green upholstery, tiny plaids of crunchy acrylics under a cottage cheese ceiling. Static electricity rose from the glinting bedspread and peppered all surfaces including my skin. This was a symptom of my allergy to normal people. I took a deep breath, settling myself. I noticed the floor lamp was the cheapest imaginable, its brass colored paint bubbled and corroded. Ludmilla stepped to the window and drew back the curtain. "You'll overlook the garden," she said hopefully.

Cool moist air enveloped my skin. Nature is so almost perfect. I saw the camellia bush right under my window, hot pink blooms amidst dark leaves that shone like washed dishes. It was one of those spring days when the dirt is swollen as a sponge and every inch is covered with soft grass. Over the course of the afternoon rain clouds had been whisked away, leaving a sky that was white and empty.

The room was 75 bucks a month for one night a week. Ludmilla promised she would empty the closet. "Okay," I said.

Our business resolved, I unpacked, and Ludmilla made tea. Then we settled down on the couch to watch her favorite show, *The Young and The Restless*. In this episode a plasticy boy was accused of raping a ghostly, miserable blond.

Ludmilla furrowed her brow at the wan blond rape victim. "Howie is a quarter of a million in debt from a gambling addiction."

"Howie? Is he your fiancé?" My voice burst out in tense girlish squeaks. Ludmilla nodded, then became pensive.

"Howie also clips articles," she said. "They puzzle me. I wonder what you would think." She went into her bedroom and brought out a brown leather box. She removed a stack of clippings, read each headline out loud and then passed the article to me.

COUPLE TENDS DEAD WOMAN AS THOUGH SHE'S ALIVE— FOR EIGHT YEARS

TODDLER KILLED BY FALLING TOMBSTONES

MAN WHO ATE NEIGHBOR'S CAT NOT PROSECUTED

Then there was a picture of a group of models with enormously long legs, posed on all fours with cages over their heads, no caption.

"What sort of person clips these?" she asked.

We mused on this subject in silence, looking at the cat-like models. Finally I said, "What do you think?"

"Well, he also walks down the street talking to himself, thinking somebody's bugged his car."

I nodded wisely. Then I excused myself and went to my new room and scribbled two lines on a piece of scrap paper:

Horror is denial at the point it turns into emotion.

I can't attach my feeling to its circumstances.

Actually there was another part to the second line, but it slipped my mind, which was probably an act of self-censorship:

Chewing the mouth of saying nothing,
in the way of that,
I can't attach my feeling to its circumstances.

One week later, on my second night at Ludmilla's, I met the Great White Hope. He walked into her apartment with an impersonal urgency, like he was late catching a train. Howie was blond and soft, almost good looking but in such a bland way it resolved into dullness. He wore a tan raincoat and khakis. Behind his wire rimmed glasses his blue eyes were watery and cold. He nodded at me briefly—actually, he barely said hello. He didn't seem to like words, and he used them sparingly, pulling his lips back from his teeth with an expression of distaste. Ludmilla hovered around him anxiously, once in a while giving me an apologetic glance. Later I heard Ludmilla and Howie having sex. Someone, I think it was Howie, bleated like a sheep.

I went to my room. I scraped my cunt until I came . . . Outside my window brilliant pink camellias nodded in the dark.

* * *

Why do I write stories that depress me? It wasn't the sound they made which was horrifying but its insignificance—so much human feeling and fantasy condensed into stuttering bleats.

Ludmilla and Howie: their wish grazes the stems of my nightmare.

Ludmilla and Howie: my nightmare grazes the stems of their idealization.

I perceive this as a problem: . . . feelings have a structure, which is not sentiment. Certain emotions are structurally sadomasochistic—for example, suspense. Even now, writing this, I feel that pained warp, as though someone whipped my brain tissues . . . Last time we had sex my beloved made me sit still, which got me so hot I could hardly stand it. It was one of those times I felt ravaged by love.

Back in the present, pared down & skimpy as a thong . . . where history comes from . . . !

I went over to Lucy's the other day. The Queens of Dope had gotten back from Italy. Where, I heard, they had been shooting heroin all day every day. I spiked with anxiety: how had they gotten the money? I wandered around Lucy's big old white house (spider sacs lining the wainscoting), and asked every girl I ran into. Each one gave me the brush-off. Finally our Italian visitor, Lidia, answered me, tossing her brown curls carelessly, "I don't know." Then she showed me the stack of counterfeit twenties she'd brought with her from Italy, and I was incredulous, actually enraged.

"Are you spending these?" I asked, furiously.

"They're all I've got." Lidia dashed away with her stash. Bills fluttered, she giggled. Then she came back. She'd stuffed her twenties someplace and now she stood awkwardly in the hallway, telling me a strange story about her mother and brother and prison and snow, walking through the mountains. There was a lot of walking through snow. The cocaine was in the kitchen and the prison was in the Italian Alps.

Are most crime stories this hard to make sense of? I expect a nudge and then knowledge, yet every story I love disappears before its end. But Lidia told me her mother was a criminal too—which made it seem solid, cultural. A Neapolitan tradition. Such familial loyalty sweetened my whole morning.

Realism infiltrates my jumpy mind. Or is it actually my *powers of reason*? Nothing is obvious among the tall trees but the sand and water provide moments of relaxation.

Narration as desire, fissure, recognition deferred via suspense so that arrival implies death . . . erosion & doubt continuing by faith collapse immediate fist. Social tissue occupied slice thinner (many pale oranges greens yellows washed together in cellular fluids) thousands of separate points woven into continuous pressure leadership.

The street hooker is the only sexually aggressive female on the street.

Trading shelter for articulation.

What we are looking for is already here, but in degraded form.

ARABIAN STUD

War party. I bring my blade.
We drink to anger, skill set collapse,
to the end of liberalism.
I feel fleshy & full of intelligence,
ready for a long ride on an Arabian stud.
. . . *an aroma of horse is a backdrop of our culture* . . .
Her thudded leg splits open
twice, over rain . . . it is a shame.
the suddenly realized weight
of the visible.

Tissues rip off that coarsened stub
as word after word slides down the throats of the Confederates.
The past is eaten by their future and becomes
futuristic cannonball
& the present, intolerable melting,
while pimping the country
to his rich friends.

War, is what. I menace. me mean. men.

When I purchased my switchblade, I bought the idea.
Now I hide it in my name.
. . . Zone of entry into eroded life,
stuck on the tip of culture
as it dries up & blows
way.

Blow.
All the needles in the forest
dipped in cocaine.
These wooden moods, with clogs:
start there, the terrific saturation of the hitch point
while the past, that girlish brainiac childhood,
pushes into my language like the ghost.
BAM BAM BAM.
If I lay down my resemblance, would it flow from me into all these guns?

Error of terror, that eye
swallowing.
All stand, scared but ready.

LUCY IN THE SKY

I put the boy to bed
turtle scout mixed from rub & spring.
Then I washed the knives, to get rid of the black stains.
There was Lucy's note, waiting
on the kitchen table.

> Dear Camille,
>
> We appear in our meat clothes and then erode. It's forty three
> by the clock. Now I've got these big boobs and a sturdy helping
> of meaty muscular. But I'm casting my ear to the winds, so to
> speak. Pulling my eyeballs out of the mud. That is personal.
> The deal with history, as I fill up my shelf, as I clutter it: my
> story will outlast the tale. The daffodils with their yellow shock,
> the mental shock of yellow upthrust from green, it's so French.
> I mean I've had this story all along and I've waited for it to
> become . . . uh, like animal skin.
>
> —Lucy

I composed a reply.

Lucy—

You were interested in lovers as dream states.
You entered the personal only through that doubt.

. . . so much tissue wasted on a dream!

LUCY
When your arms crunched my ribs,
holes opened up in my psyche
& I was spongy & clear . . .
LUCY
with the big eraser,
all my feelings
turning
vapor—

Each of your gifts, we hauled across the plateau:
such as a light cunt, lightened by aperture.
And something we were letting coil in our ears, those pushy disturbances.

Now I feel, uh, wedded to evil. My brain keeps serving up nasty pop-tarts
in which peace of mind is indicated by bubbles of lust.
What you & I did was so good it was nauseating.
xox
Camille

Dear Camille,

Happy about your note. I didn't expect it. It's weird, that moment of being sexually attracted to someone who might be dead. You weren't the first. When N. died, I loved her desperately, my feverish hands closing over a ghost.

Last night's bath left my scalp itchy. This morning the view out the kitchen window down to the port (factories and warehouses) was of a dreamy peachy pink sky over the glossy bay. The colors were so pretty they whirred.

I'm sick of being here, in pretty-land.

Bad sex. Abusive sex. Kinky sex. Established sex. Tunnel of love sex. Buried muscles in chalk. Big toe in a bottle, buried again.
You can imagine my amazement when I heard you were not dead!
Your living warmth made me sleepy. I slept for four days.
Love, Lucy

Dear Lucy,
I'm rattled. Every night a different rattle.
Every day, waiting.

This may be the weekend he dies. They're all gathering.

His knees are bigger than his thighs. He weighs 95 pounds. He's covered with lesions. He crawls around the house and if we don't watch him there's shit everywhere.

Today the boy woke up early & came down my stairs crying
Where are the clouds?
It was before dawn and the sky was white.

Lucy, our frantic episode was undercut by embarrassment.
Surrealism and embarrassment and a humor like heated fur.
It resembled a meditation but was more painful. It was romance.
Slowly rags crushed their paws into my chest.
Lungs bleated while the aroma seeped from my nipples.
I was still singing, *Can this go on?*
while sitting cross-legged among the stinky pillows.
Dear Lucy, your body is judicious . . .

Baffled reader of my own life!
Camille

Dear Camille,
I read somewhere that dialog is tongues-in-a-nest.

My tongue is wagging in my stomach & it wants to be scooped
    out. For a cluster fuck.
A closure fuck. A placement.
As you press your palm to the mirror of my face,
I'll have nothing to say to that palm.
We'll practice breathing as you deviously surround my nipples
    with tiny barracuda.
Tunnel of air is all I'll have to kiss you with. I'll be nude then!
Camille—I need your brainy ideas because . . . because I'm . . .
You are supposed to love me particularly, to pluck my plum.
    To wet fur me aside.
Everyone else was just a sex toy.
(My pants need gathering & squishing.)

pleadingly,
Lucy

Dear Lucy,
I calm myself with magazines.
Stare at you from the greatest distance I can imagine.
Your hands cup my tremble and I could piss
just from relief. That's my feeling.
It's invented & pleasurable & underage.

Tiny tongue marches in the welt
then whiplash. The joke stares before jumping.

Or something! Stuffed with plans and paranoia . . .

This is what I'll do:
I'll gather my interests into a Herd,
& head for that valley of blood known as the brain.
I'll drag myself to the shore, flop by the water, suck a bottle of soda.
I'll feel so complete, sunning at the beach next to my own guilty corpse
wherein appetites fester.
Giving you up . . .
            . . . a waffle between flattery and substance.
Opening my life to what's intelligible!

I always wanted to be a gangster but I guess I'm just a punk.
still yours, Camille

Dear Camille,
So many little scams—out in the world, etcetera.
Who cares! I think about our slinking attraction,
everyone ignores it if they can. But it's the nugget of our story.

Did I tell you what your boy said when I took him to the fireworks?
The adventure is in the sky. The adventure is falling down.

I thought you were the white legs in the grass
gleaming & moonlit. Seeping their whiteness.
You were my miniature city
but this room is my hole, with its greasy sheets
& queasy fantasies (slick this ending with regret).

I took a mud bath & understood what was so great about being
    an earthworm
with no problems & a brain as pure as a cloud.
If emotions aren't reality, what is?

Goodbye, architecture of my life—
love, Lucy

LA FICA È SACRA

Once we have understood how it develops minute personal
failings into public crimes, then nothing is a minute
personal failing. One's little faults can only be crimes.
—Simone Weil

sex like an orange lining. sex like tubs. sex like glazing. sex like pan
fried. sex like lettuce crisp. sex like tea. sex like waiting. sex like
cotton dyes.

I stroke the stack of bills because they are soft
& smell like lanolin: modesty in a stack of twenties
as the counterfeiter Lidia teaches me the Italian for
The Pussy Is Sacred.

Then Scout snickers as she studies my prospects:
No $ + no audience + anxiety = sin.

(Scout's not the fiction but
volumes of violent death
& what is weird
is being inside—pouched—
submerged, invisible.
Some day Scout will reject me &
then I will be *as if* dead . . .

Her religious family having been stunned into bitterness.

. . . So much for the wish that spills,
or the pain which is a consequence of walking upright.
Now Scout's a scab
of herself, a thickening
swab of narrative texture. Tearing it up
into this poem . . . I desire that character
like a novel!)

I show Scout the rejection letter
        . . . *We are looking for restraint in the interest of refinement* . . .

Then we're back to our subject: where we went,
fields of battle bitterly regarded
as each grain moves from nostril to atmosphere.

I confess my dream: I molested Lucas' apartment, where I found
        one of my scripts,
which Lucas had marked up with a red editor's pen.
At the end he'd scribbled this:

> *Toil in the fields black as rotted bark.*
> *Raise an army of rapists. Beat the children.*
> *In the wicked tree of the wicked, you're my favorite.*

Scout thinks the Lucas *aroma of dangerousness* is merely
a consequence of early success.
In his twenties Lucas was oddly middle-aged (a lump) letting go with
one or the other gulps in the middle of the fight.
Whereas I locate disgust: where it goes, I go

with the dictator's ambition: to smash the rules which would
    judge me
into minute patterns, like truths.
Grains begin in the dark pads of flesh.
Today a single new style has come into existence
stressing frank use of metal
a visible articulation of the skeleton.
Of course the dictator's big shits intimidate me.

Resistance gathers yet won't speak.

Questions are anathema.

HISTORY OF THE SLUT
IN MY RELATIONSHIP

In the kitchens of love, after all, vice is like the pepper in a
good sauce; it brings out the flavor, it's indispensable.
—Céline

The problem with sex is that it fires the harder life.

It all happened in one week.
What?   1. trip to the police station.
                  2. sex, sex.
                  3. the dream of the movie theater.

Then the red minx curled up,
lashing her outward parts.
Chest high knobs with soft tips,
twitchy in the deep cups of her bra,
conveyed nothing other than the angelic—that *blank*.
A solution proffered by the beloved, in all ways
wise because of a crack in her head:
  • her delightful monster of a body
  • the thumb prints
on her eyelids.

A description of her. *red minx*. is a description
of the representational boundary.

One big surprise in the dark!

Afterwards she disappeared.

then I found a disposable camera under the bed.
Got it developed: smiling yellow
     Pictures of her wedding!

Whereas this talk show desire of mine is in the field—
          'I'm v. interested in
          slut head trips,
          both agonizing & amusing:
          what works in the world of the slut
          for my book: *The Friendly Slut.*'

That sentence
is a sort of dildo
which
language for me permeable to loss
as I have lost one (language) (at least)
I skim the surface of that absence of memory.
I think it makes my usage more violent.
So, my exile is limited in scope.
So my tongue, so my lips
placed with the luggage.

You sexually learn to widen the acceptable . . .
my sort of spreading butt.

Not for me the scandalous appetites nor shining body—

WANTING TO REGISTER IN THE ROAD & THE CHARACTERISTICS OF THE REAL

The rich don't have to kill to eat.
They "employ" people, as they call it.
—Céline

The circular flakes,
unable to register.

So I begat toleration,
then. That girl named Toleration
and her fake brushes.
Whose body, once built,
yielded a pound of sweats, drained.

I made a special trip to hear her piss.
(The strip club toilet was wired.)

Out in the real world. uneven & dusty.
two boys walk down the road.
They bend and grimace in the heat. Because its wartime
they're my boys, somehow. Whoa!

"I've heard little bags contain teeth and pills
also
secret forms of prostitution."
White teeth rattle in my ironic mouth.
I tell them the girl had an unusual
booze style, hard-edged but elegant. Always
having a reservoir of brutality:
more in the tank.

Nodding, in the breath of gun.
My wide angle lens catches their hysteria:
my boys screaming, falling

In the deep with guns being traded . . .
In the tumult of sunshine & growth . . . In the organ
that sheds thoughts . . . fiction. Guns
being traded?

Secrecy presents with a form of discipline,
an illness of the spine, in which my nerves carry odd
even uncanny pains.

EMBARRASSED TRACT

In memory of J.W.

At the edge of wilderness: agriculture. Out back I'm happy with
    the smell of plum
and soiled texture. There's a rocking oil rig, phallic thumb sticking
    in dirt. Everything's
impossibly green, except where black. Inside her husband weeps
    and rocks
on his rotten feet.

Couch depth.
I pass the white plate, its neat helping, its help.

The family hog rolls in glue
as we sit in a circle
dazed.
Getting older we ponder
creamer, creamsicle, cremation:
Hello Big Farmer,
I like your bottomless pot.

Our family is sexed, plethora of the gash. Together forever, we'll
     slide through the past,
greasy at the rim, through the critical discourse that we use.
Dear dead: What about
the vigor of the impersonal, that mansion without a suspect—
is it comfortable?

—I don't know what to do with the money.
—Good thing there isn't any.
—She fell and the tissue sheared red.
(Oops, the end.)
—Witch of the hours of bleeding and rot: Her nail ghost widened
     the road,
shaming a lot
of pleasures from poetry.

A ghost escapes circumstances; that is what a ghost is.
Plot-scandal. The cartoons dangle.
The problem is timing.

KEEPING A CHEWY GRIPPE

Stick a lemon in the ground.
Sleep on it.

This is our dark, said the beautiful gangster from Texas.
'FUCK BUSH' was blazing on his t-shirt.

Tower of criminal brotherhood!
Annals of true crimes: because
the body *is* good looking
it carries a charge.

Erotic dust, shaken off.
Each poetic clump, when it arrives,
is accompanied by disgust. Is
it personal? Where

is the poem? It dies as a part of me. Expelled.
Sort of . . . like shitting.

His girlfriend, red minx
& muscular as a ferret, is pleasing also.

THE ROYAN HOTEL

To Pimp Across Texas
is a chain of pancake restaurants
in which Lonnie got fat
and Jewel shone
cruel
& flagrant.
A good body supposedly *holds* the baby.
But the day Jewel went out
she attached to the world through that image.
Now she's a
splinter a sphincter
dusk
swallowing air—
while Lonnie, all those tattoos,
he looks like he's wearing a rug.

Haiku smashes the current of exegesis.
I find myself
—perfect—
—a missing limb—
—dried figment—
. . . the throb detective in the diorama,
I'm <u>that</u>.
My phantom finger leads the way,
its shadow wobbling.
" . . . After five more chemotherapy treatments at Starbucks
                    I'll be fine."

Rosie—I knew her way back,
before motherhood or her T.V. show.
One day in a diner Rosie told me
she'd been kidnapped by aliens & sexually abused.
I dug it. Dug out.

>   *Canoes glide into the orchard, under stars.*

Rosie, come in please.
Through your character, that shuddering wave,
a light pierces my pinhole camera.
Your sullen, soiled motherhood
with little pests
(I'm waiting for it).

Poems dig up solids
or simply don't
die after vomiting blood.
Jewel looked asleep in her scuffed and tropical satin.
I heard Lonnie was dead too but he reappeared missing a finger.
Maybe the reincarnate was his bounce back:
Pow, then minxes and ghosts.

GOLDEN SYRUP

Except for the ruddy tips on his cheeks
Nico is soft and white: a boy consumed by his tender wrapping.
"I am a lucky person," he announces. "I can trust my instincts."

Seated across the table, two very fat women look suspiciously at us.
Is that a coldness in the culture?
clumped. Their disgust
at these impersonal rushes—
My pleasure of walking in the shimmer, as it walks away with me

while at home, my beloved waits, with her big arms and flat waist.

I smooth out her letter,
dazzled at first, then morose, as I remember my grudge.
Attitude is the force that keeps me speaking,
filling the wounded office.
What flows out of me comes up through my feet, from the earth.
My job is to conceal this.
Objects—like masks—with smiles,
I carry off & arrange.

Nico is the sun, over this upset.
He gossips about Anne, in her 'love slave' phase:
she's happily available, only for breakfast.
(Her confinement means she knows where she is
though it takes quite a lot of effort.)

Our tea is scented with bourbon roses.
Nico's short black hair is cut like a cap,
& neatly trimmed at the neck

whereas I'm mean as a dream and clean without tonguing the woods.
Tired of scribblings I want themes:
soft flesh to twist my nails in

or a slogan, 'White people are shits.'

COLD VIRGINS (A SAD SONG)

For an inmate poetry class at a California prison

A man on the bus leaned into me
pressing the ax in his paper bag against my leg.
On his other side a woman gasped and pressed
her palms to her face: 2 warm circles of skin.
Then a man jumped up and apologized, "For all men."

Expectation spreads the rug, paranoia butters it.
All strung & played, with severe handicaps,
pancake girl shoots up in the echo chamber.
It's not even disappointing:
the crush of my whole life.

The boy who keeps crimes as pets,
3 melodious girls who dip teaspoons into sugar—
their disturbance is present in every part of the action.
Every day I wait for their return,
getting by on loyalty
& transportation into the ether of my own tones.

A life of crime, always in tatters, is hard work.
I'm restless to put my fist inside that pit stop.
Dear prisoners, who have lived a little,
my hips are solid as my stew pot . . .
It's the creativity of emptiness (again).

Leadership creates a vacuum
filled by followers:
blue vaults of the sky.
We must be continuous now,
having just come out of the vault.

LUCKY FORTUNE IS GOOD

Dear One
This is what I heard: after desire replaced God
you reentered painting through the back door of advertising
in shiny proliferation of dime bags & divine strut.

Dear One
Everyone knows
paradise was soiled by God's excrement—secretive twins,
who fell to the ground in sullen lumps,
to be wrapped in woolen coats & trampled.
Then language entered them: a black food.
Boy absorbed boy, so the girl wandered
away & became
a bird.

Dear One
Now the girl wants to know:
if there's no tradition of good,
is she allowed to rely on luck?

About the Poet
Also, the girl became a poet, scratching out—evil but innocent—
succinct predators.

A Poem
Along the wide southbound turn
a hawk floats over the road's thin fringe of grass.

A knife glints.
In the reddish dirt
the girl's scraped &
dazzled knees.
Her eyes swallowing dark.
She snatches the gift
then
my mother hitched to Kentucky and after that
to Portsmouth, Maine, to meet a sailor.
My mother was fifteen.
In my dream two shaggy black pelts
came out of my sides, above my hip bones.
They were long so
I clipped them.
As I did,
I heard my mother singing . . .
'When such as I cast out remorse
So great a sweetness flows into the breast . . . '
I admit to relying on luck.
It feels woody, or else
that's the prickly smell
(like rough sheets) . . .

Dear One
Which word begins the austere touch of your poem?
Or is it true
that *silence is doubt* . . .
Silence soaked into the rock.
Is that your language?

                              (for Larry Friedlander)

FILM LOOP

A film is a real long thing . . . a compendium of feeling.
—Arnold Kemp

The scientist, eyes pinned, crawls around his lab
collecting all the broken test tubes
as the girl sleeps peacefully on her concrete block.
She's stolen everything he can't find—
his pills, his private complaints, his basic
measure of no resemblance—
even the dead boy in a circular gown
whose pale beauties
silky colors, ripples—
the icicle skirt.

Crime: the ecstasy of the rule.
Its moral is our instruction.
Wrapped in gray silk, lips slightly parted,
the girl lies as still as a corpse—
To marry in the ecstasy of theory,
& apply crime to your life.
She'll share our disassociative trick
of participating in suffering without experiencing it . . .

You yanked the weeds this afternoon.
I smell mint still on your knuckles.
The night is a warm tub we cuddle in
as the reels sputter
Horror In Egypt
& the girl appears again,
veiled, staggering.

PRINCESS & SALT (A BALLAD)

All night I spent on my knees
munching the feminine.
2 distinct occurrences in the dark
dream girls, separated
by blur.

Finally day broke. You know what I mean?
And they spent the morning washing,
Princess & Salt. So much white,
bleached sheets flowing
out of the tubs.

Glittering & weeded

                  laconic Salt. Chosen,
      emptied. My black-eyed star.
(I found out one of my dream girls was a boy.)
And Princess: A tiny doll
sucks her shoulder
Her bones snap
       as she walks.   Rat-a-tat-tat.
          Ankles screwy like that.
Love-soaked sweetheart
slutty girl, leaving shiny paths.
What a dream
this trail she's following. Mucked up
alleys & streets, a bowl
of languages, smells

63

of baking fortune cookies & mineral salts.

Waves big as dinosaurs

rise up from her comic book, it's Japanese
lots of porn w/ semi-delirious violence.
Dream boy Salt has girlish lips
pouts up from the page,
one foot on the prow
& hand to sword
glaring.
Salt hates her
Wrong: he loves her with a criminal love
laying throb next to blade
explaining tools
the shootings.
Then he curls up
under the newspapers, crying and relaxing.

Leaving her breathing upstairs, going down
Princess lays her head on Salt's shoulder.
Chilly wedge. Blood sours &
moves slowly, a paste
warmed where bodies fill with light.
Days like that.
They had to break some fingers.
Managed to pull Princess back.

Lucy thinks guilt must belong somewhere:
there's always a supplier
(of guilt, if nothing else). But I think
bodies are stubborn.
Piling on top of one another   simply for warmth.

PROPERTIES OF CRIMINAL GIRLS IN THE STRING UNIVERSE

Camping at Hendy Woods, Northern California

The car in a ditch. The kids snacking on potato chips.
Hiking for a phone, I pass a large snake coiled on the warm
    black asphalt.
She shakes her rattle at me, glides into dry grass.
Green & black diamonds
glide into the grass.
Then the very nice tow truck driver Robert
drives me to the river.
His wife, he explains, is a walking meth corpse in Mississippi.

On the one hand, a sense of cartoonishly re-imagined memoir . . .
    on the other, a body
with a surprising stride & swish . . .

"A secret of life is that it's fine to be dead. Getting there is
    the problem,"

says Bob, being Bob, in the arc of Bob,
riding to the place of higher love

snow in the pistons,
smashed repeatedly.

Big: I've had one dream only, the others are breaths in & out of
the body of my bigger dream. Streams of excited electrons—
but only one throb.

Little: a mouse with a sequined tutu, a dragon beanie, a hairless
monkey & a hairy one. Sequined butterflies which flutter
towards universal love.

Out of scale, yet within view:
A candle lantern dangles from blue lampshade sky.
In a hot tented pavilion, next to the red tank (with shiny mineral
scum floating on the water)
I reflect upon Lucy. Her crimes
slide out of my grasp & dissolve further downstream.
My frank disapproval, which is empty I guess
since the freaks around here
still line up at the back door with stuff to sell:
A bike, backpack, a torn screen door,
a paint spattered radio.

TODAY

Today, a day without writing
as the city turns into flame.
An apparition in the desert: a palm stalk
where there was another expectation.
"We can't become our culture
when it abandons us."
We swelter the long walk to the river,
our memory of which is sky
hurtling into non-sky,
robes of wind & ice crystals.
This rubble is justice passing.

TORTURE IN DAPPLE

The rich torture in dapple
their furtive milk as musk groves
or chain mail
weep
selfishly
until finally dry.

Hey, luscious scab,
where's my fiction?

// Ride it like a donkey
// Push it like a broom
// Inside chambers of meat
// A body has its limits.

Poetry for the churning
pain in my brain.
. . . Call it Lucy, plump & alien,
the dear scar
which is what my life has given me:
honesty
contracted like tribal skin;
contracted loyalty for passage
towards death.

I probably owe you money.

Humor is noise twisted into emotion,
scratched into the husk.

SING SONG

I flew
into
that deep crack.
No one anywhere all lights out
& thugs: their
flushed sadism buds melted
by beer.
Through an unlatched door, into a cellar
through smells of rotted vegetables and gasoline,
sandals
stop.
Chased into an empty world.

Later: I opened the door and saw Katerina's fleshy shoulders rise
from the claw foot tub. Her skin was a raised surface of tiny bumps.
"A rash," she said. She was in her nightly bath, steam filling the living
room. That was the year Katerine leaned towards me, absorbent,
mimicking my gestures, style, my American slang.

(Did I tell her? I don't remember.
Because my toes were too big. *Swatted, stomped.*)

A year of her leaning towards me, in agreement
(ice in her throat)
while I hoped something would be recovered.
But Katarine was indifferent
because our association began before criticism.

Now, as minutes push against my body (disintegrate into paper strips)
softly chewing wood pulp
I dream I kiss Kevin Killian.

Over and over, I have sex
with one person
under a blanket of insult.
The toad between my legs
hops & hardly tires me:
Sing, song, slut.

ARTIFACT

Scott is such an imp, for an old thug. He sparkles, it's the way he talks, jumpy & gymnastic. His hands float up. As we walk down the windy street, past apartments grimy with auto exhaust, he presses his hands into that bud shape. "The lotus blooms at night, in swamps and filth," he tells me, batting his eye lashes. This is how a religion inspires love, I think.

I follow him to his Tibetan group. There are hardly any Tibetans but lots of paintings of hell.

"Life is hell," Scott likes to say, passionately.

The room is small with hot reddish colors. & hangings of swirling radiant figures set into fields of degradation & crime.

. . . Karma-Krodhisvari is clasping his body with her right arm, her hand around his neck, and in her left she is holding a blood-filled skull to his lips . . .

There are high hard cushions in rows on woven mats. Scott chooses one, sitting cross-legged, poised & mesmerized. I have a cramp in my leg almost instantly. The seconds etch through my cramp until finally a bell ends the sitting. Scott wants to go to the Starbucks on the corner. Its fuzzy Parisian scenes are scraped with graffiti: ill legiblah lotto, @why.

Poetry is kind of violence . . .
Spasm as lyricism
of origin and transformational power.
A main purpose of the state is to break down the gang by offering
its members something in exchange: rights as a citizen.
The Law shines over the herd.

" . . . Almost all dead." Scott is speaking. Only two of the living are not incarcerated: Scott and some actor in Los Angeles.

As Scott talks, he's witnessing, & I am thrust in his life. We have some affinity that's bloody—genetic. Back in the swarm of old Kentucky days we gnawed on the same bone . . . Now isn't that a strange thing to think. I must be in a mood. It's the methods he tells me about. Though they're not the point. The information hurts my tissues. The air I breathe contains it. Scott leans back, dazed. Smell of black coffee on his breath.

Of course Scott was practically a kid but that's not the point either. Work makes the world in exactly this way: artifact. Thin lines of life & death compose it. Murder is somebody's job. Just not mine.

PARADE

To write is to kill.
—Blanchot

The chase is on as I imitate gestures,
this time I'm following a large & perfect man.
Dear Succulent:
meat in kindly stripes.

With the excitement of being among men but inside the women

my history floats down the avenue
in blobs / atomic
landfill—that
purse & its abstraction,
the empty suit.
Revenge is a character who suffered
& became chronic.
I call her
Hotel Paranoia: *"Get to bed
on time!*
If you want to have sex."

Now that I'm so close to the street,
being *on* the street,
purple in the street,
fried street,
I can delete embarrassment at the level of structure.

(oh fluttering fans!)

I love the cloud
around speech
we call the body . . .
House of sensation.
Built crud wrapper.

"But what about those Russians, *they're* not slouched
in the bed of fake trauma . . .
Not yet.
. . . Not in the pleasure sense—No."

NOTES ON THE MANUSCRIPT

(1) Céline epigraph for poem "Ideology," page 5, from "Journey to the End of Night," page 188, New Directions; Third printing edition (May 17, 2006).

(2) Simone Weil quote in poem "Boxy," page 9, from "Gravity and Grace," page 181, Routledge; New edition (November 12, 2002).

(3) Simone Weil epigraph for poem "La Figa È Sacra," page 44, from "First and Last Notebooks" R. Rees (Translator), page 346, Oxford University Press (July 2, 1970).

(4) Céline epigraph for poem "History Of The Slut In My Relationship," page 46, from above book, page 51.

(5) Céline epigraph for poem "Wanting to register in the road & the characteristics of the real," page 48, from above book, page 287.

(6) W. B. Yeats embedded quote in poem "Lucky Fortune is Good," page 59, from "A Dialogue of Self and Soul" in The Collected Poems of W.B. Yeats, Wordsworth Editions Ltd (November 5, 1994).

(7) Arnold Kemp epigraph for poem "Film Loop," page 61, from a poem by Arnold Kemp, with the title (at the time, since changed) "Moments Before a Complete Concordance." It is currently unpublished.

(8) La Fica È Sacra, page 66, phrases taken from "The International Style" by H. R. Hitchcock & Philip Johnson (1932), current edition W. W. Norton & Company (February 17, 1997).

CREDITS

Earlier versions of some of these poems appeared previously,
as listed below:

- Eoagh #3: "Katerine," "Affiliated."
- Outlet #4/5: "Mechanical Bride."
- Shampoo #22: "Tower Hotel."
- Shampoo #29: "La Fica È Sacra."
- ambit #2.2: "Parade" (editor kari edwards).
- Pom²: "Arabian Stud," "Embarrassed Tract."
- Belladonna Chapbook #2: "Reverse History," "Dream Girls."
- Satellite Telephone #1: "Sacrifice," "Today."
- Tantalum #1: "Crime Story."
- poetz / 'for immiediate release' "Snow Instruction"
  (editor kari edwards).
- The Book of Practical Pussies, Michelle Rollman, artist: "History
  of the Slut in My Relationship." Krupskaya 2009.
- Bay Area Poetics, Faux Press, 2006, editor Stephanie Young:
  "Boxy," "Good Body," "My Play."

This book was set in Sabon, an old style serif typeface designed by Jan Tschichold in 1967 and used, among other things, for the 1979 Book of Common Prayer.

This first edition, first printing includes 26 limited edition copies lettered A-Z and sigend by the author.